A VISION OF
SNOWDONIA

JERRY RAWSON

HALSGROVE

First published in Great Britain in 2008

Title page: The moon rises across a misty Llynnau Mymbyr at dawn backed by the Snowdon range.

Right: The cascades of Rhaeadr-fawr – usually known as Aber Falls – situated on the northern slopes of the Carneddau near Abergwyngregyn.

British Library Cataloguing-in-Publication Data
A CIP record for this title is available from the British Library

ISBN 978 1 84114 769 7

HALSGROVE
Halsgrove House, Ryelands Industrial Estate,
Bagley Road, Wellington, Somerset TA21 9PZ
Tel: 01823 653777   Fax: 01823 216796
email: sales@halsgrove.com
website: www.halsgrove.com

Printed and bound by Everbest Printing Co. Ltd, China

INTRODUCTION

However many times I travel west along the A4086 from Capel Curig I never tire of the scene that suddenly opens up of the Snowdon range across Llynnau Mymbyr just past Plas y Brenin (The National Mountain Centre). Seen at dawn or dusk with the Snowdon massif reflected in the mirror-like surface of the lake, this is one of the iconic views in the Snowdonia National Park.

The Snowdonia National Park – Parc Cenedlaethol Eryri – lies in the north-west of Wales and contains some of the most spectacular and tightly packed mountain scenery in the United Kingdom. Established in 1951 as the third National Park in England and Wales it covers an area of 827 sq miles (2142sq km) and has 37 miles (60km) of coastline. It is a land of heather moors, lakes, wooded valleys, dramatic coastlines with great sweeping bays, and craggy mountain ranges. You cannot escape the sea in Snowdonia and almost every mountain top offers you glimpses of it.

With such diverse scenery it's not surprising that Snowdonia offers an unending variety of interest for photographers. Each season has its own beauty – from the purple-clad heather moors above Bala in high summer; the golden autumnal colours of the ancient woods around Dolgellau; the vast arctic-like plateau of the Carneddau; the impressive snow-covered ridges and cwms of the Snowdon massif, with Yr Wyddfa, at 3560ft (1085m), the highest point in England and Wales. Snowdonia's magnificent landscape also attracts walkers and offers some great mountain days including the classic Snowdon Horseshoe and the north ridge of Tryfan.

This book explores the valleys and hills, seeking out summits and lakes, which together make Snowdonia such a very special place. I always enjoy the ever-changing terrain with its rocky ridges leading up to isolated mountain summits; dramatic ice-carved cwms and hidden lakes; huge whaleback ridges and open moorland; the magical light and those amazing colour changes through the seasons.

Over the last few decades Snowdonia has provided me with endless photographic opportunities and challenges. I use various cameras and format sizes but for this book the images are presented in 3:1 ratio panoramic format. This wider view creates a different perspective of the landscape and emphasises the rugged beauty of Snowdonia.

Photographing this amazing landscape can be very rewarding but also requires great patience, and a strong back for carrying all the photographic equipment and tripod. It can be quite frustrating waiting on the top of a peak for the sun to rise only to find a bank of cloud rolling in from the east blocking out the magical dawn light or sheltering behind rocks waiting for heavy rain to pass over and, one hopes, leave storm clouds and dramatic light. The best photographic conditions are mostly around dawn and dusk when the light can be a revelation, transforming even a mundane landscape into something quite sublime.

The choice of pictures and their order is purely personal but hopefully my selection conveys the beauty and atmosphere of this landscape, maybe encouraging readers to go and discover the area for themselves. I apologise if your favourite location has been left out.

Jerry Rawson

ACKNOWLEDGEMENTS
I would like to thank my wife Katy for her help, support, and patience, during the production of this book.

Carneddau wilderness
A bright and breezy day follows a snow shower on Bera Mawr and Llwytmor seen from the rocky top of Bera Bach. This area is at the quieter northern end of the Carneddau range.

Cwm Eigiau
A farm track leads the
eye towards the remote
Cwm Eigiau, on the eastern
flanks of the Carneddau.

Bluebells
Bluebells in the Conwy Valley herald the arrival of spring.

Shapely peak
The pyramidal-shaped Pen yr Ole Wen, which has one of the steepest ascents in the Carneddau, dominates this view across the Ogwen Valley seen from the outflow of Llyn Idwal.

Overlooking Tryfan
The top of Bristly Ridge
on Glyder Fach provides
a great viewpoint over
the shapely cone of Tryfan to
the southern Carneddau.

Cwm Lloer
A boulder acts as a foreground in this stunning winter view of Cwm Lloer and Pen yr Ole Wen from the Ogwen Valley.

Overleaf:
Pink dawn
As the weak winter sun crests the surrounding hills the warming dawn light turns the veils of mist pink in this westerly view through the Ogwen Valley.

Ogwen Valley
A classic early morning spring-time view through the Ogwen Valley showing Glyder Fach, Tryfan, Y Garn and Pen yr Ole Wen.

Overleaf:
Alpenglow
Dawn light picks out the impressive rocky buttresses on the east face of Tryfan, and its neighbour Glyder Fach, seen across Cwm Tryfan from the ridge of Braich y Ddeugwm.

Sunset over Tryfan
The wonderful colours of a
summer sunset are captured
over the wedge-shaped Tryfan
backed by the Glyderau.

Pinnacled Ridge
Glyder Fach rises beyond Llyn y Caseg-fraith. The pinnacled and craggy northern spur of Glyder Fach, known as Bristly Ridge, is visible on the right-hand skyline.

Splintered rocks
The moon rises beyond splintered rocks on Castell y Gwynt.

Castle of the Winds
Castell y Gwynt (castle of the winds) forms a dramatic foreground
for this view of Glyder Fawr and the Snowdon range.

Erosion
A cluster of eroded rocks on the summit slopes of Glyder Fach act as a foreground in this view of Glyder Fawr, Y Garn and Foel Goch.

Dusk silhouette
A stunning sunset beyond the silhouetted splintered crest of Castell y Gwynt (castle of the winds) near the summit of Glyder Fach and backed by Glyder Fawr (right) and the Snowdon range.

Morning reflections
An early morning view of
Y Garn reflected in the calm
waters of Llyn Ogwen.

Winter morning
Tryfan, in its winter raiment,
looks quite alpine in this view
from the west near Llyn Ogwen.

Lone tree
A lone tree acts as a focal point in this springtime view across Cwm Idwal to Y Garn.

Overleaf:
Erratic boulder
A glacial erratic boulder acts as a foreground for this dawn view into the impressive glacier-carved Cwm Idwal, with the cleft of Twll Du (Devil's Kitchen), visible in the craggy head wall of the cwm.

Ogwen Valley
Y Garn provides a bird's-eye-view of Llyn Ogwen in the Ogwen Valley, with Tryfan on the right and Pen yr Ole Wen to the left.

Idwal Slabs
An unusual perspective of Idwal Slabs and the buttresses of Glyder Fawr overlook Cwm Idwal in this view from the slopes of Y Garn. The easy-angled slabs have been a playground for generations of rock climbers.

Overleaf:
Nant Ffrancon
The slopes of Pen yr Ole Wen offer a great view of the deep trench of the Nant Ffrancon, a classic glacial trough over-looked by the craggy slopes of Foel Goch.

Rising mist
The dawn sunshine warms up the foreground rocks as mist rises from the surface of Llynnau Mymbyr near Capel Curig.

Pointed peak
The lower slopes of Glyder Fawr offer a fine view across Llanberis Pass to the shapely peak of Crib Goch.

Overleaf:
The Snowdon Horseshoe
A view across Crib Goch Pinnacles backed by Carnedd Ugain and pointed Yr Wyddfa (Snowdon) at the start, or finish, of the classic Snowdon Horseshoe circuit.

Across Cwm Uchaf
A patch of sunlight picks out the celebrated Crib Goch Pinnacles soaring up above red-coloured screes in this view across Cwm Uchaf from near the summit of Carnedd Ugain.

Overleaf:
Dawn light
The dramatic east-facing cliffs of Y Lliwedd rearing up above Llyn Llydaw look spectacular captured in warm, dawn light in this view from the slopes of Crib Goch.

Boulders

A cluster of boulders in Cwm Dyli create a pleasing foreground for this view of the pointed summit of Snowdon (Yr Wyddfa), at 3560ft/ 1085m, the highest point in England and Wales.

Dusk
The sun sets beyond the Snowdon hills in this classic view into Cwm Dyli across Llynnau Mymbyr, near Capel Curig.

Llyn Llydaw
Y Lliwedd and Yr Wyddfa
(Snowdon) stand proud in
this classic early morning
view across Llyn Llydaw with
the slopes of Crib Goch
on the right.

Y Wyddfa

A striking springtime view of the pyramid-shaped Yr Wyddfa (Snowdon) seen from the shores of Llyn Llydaw. The ruins of the Britannia Copper Works can be seen across the lake.

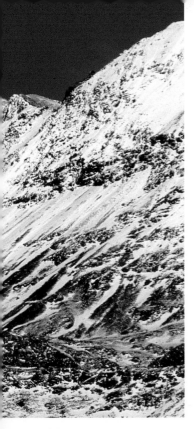

Winter cloak
The majestic bulk of Yr Wyddfa
under its winter mantle overlooks
Cwm Dyli with Carnedd Ugain
and Crib Goch to the right.

The morning after

After a heavy overnight snowfall, weak sunshine highlights the shapely peak of Crib Goch, the first summit on the classic Snowdon Horse-shoe. Seen in its full glory stretching from Crib Goch to Y Lliwedd, this circuit is a challenging winter expedition for mountaineers.

Sunrise over Snowdon
Dawn light illuminates the
tops of the Snowdon range
in this classic view across
Nant Gwynant.

Winter giants
Veils of mist swirl around the
snowy summits of Snowdon
(Yr Wyddfa) and Crib Goch,
which in conditions like these
look like Himalayan giants.

The Pass
Looking west down the
deep trench of Llanberis
Pass from the slopes of
Glyder Fawr near Pen y Pass.

Llyn Padarn
A combination of setting sun and atmospheric storm clouds create a dramatic view across Llyn Padarn, near Llanberis, with the Snowdon hills as a backdrop.

Overleaf:
The Black Cliff
The huge precipices of Clogwyn Du'r Arddu – The Black Cliff – guard Snowdon's northern flanks. Cloggy, with its impressive rock architecture, is one of Britain's premier climbing venues.

Moel Cynghorion
One of the northern outlying
peaks of the Snowdon massif
is the shapely Moel Cynghorion
seen here in this view across
Cwm Brwnynog from below
Clogwyn Du'r Arddu.

Winter sunset
An amazing scene as the sun sets beyond the Snowdon hills reflected in Llynnau Mymbyr seen from Royal Bridge near Capel Curig.

Sentinel tree
A solitary tree acts as a focal point in this winter view across Nant Gwynant to Crib Goch.

Overleaf:
Yr Aran
Trees and the smooth-surfaced Llyn Gwynant act as a beautiful foreground for the isolated and shapely peak of Yr Aran, an outlier on the south ridge of Snowdon.

Moel Hebog
The shapely peak of Moel
Hebog soars above Beddgelert
in this beautiful winter morning
view along Nant Gwynant.

Tranquillity
Trees reflected in the mirror-like surface of Llyn Gwynant near Beddgelert.

Overleaf:
Last light
As the sun dips below the horizon the final light illuminates the hills west of Cnicht seen here reflected in the calm surface of Llyn Dinas near Beddgelert.

Reeded lake
Reeds on the shore of Llyn y Gader near Rhyd Ddu provide a foreground for this view of Y Garn (left) and Mynydd Mawr.

Overleaf:
Llyn Cwellyn
The lower section of the Snowdon Ranger track up Snowdon provides an excellent view across Llyn Cwellyn. The lake lies beside the road from Beddgelert to Caernarfon, and is overlooked by the whaleback hill of Mynydd Mawr (right) with Y Garn visible on the skyline to the left.

Storm over Rhyd Ddu
Approaching storm clouds sweep across Y Garn and the Nantlle Ridge (left), Mynydd Mawr (right) and the village of Rhyd Ddu.

Becalmed
Three rowing boats on a mirror-like Llyn y Dywarchen near Rhyd Ddu.

Overleaf:
After the storm
A combination of snow-shower clouds and spring sunshine create a wonderful view across Llyn y Dywarchen near Rhyd Ddu, to the western flanks of Snowdon.

Llyn Nantlle Uchaf
Reflections and the last light of the setting sun create a peaceful view across Llyn Nantlle Uchaf to a snow-capped Snowdon wedged between Mynydd Mawr on the left and Y Garn to the right.

Overleaf:
The Moelwyn hills
Dark clouds pass over Moelwyn Mawr (left) and Moelwyn Bach (right) separated by the craggy top of Craigysgafn in this excellent view from the west above the village of Croesor.

Storm over Cnicht

Storm clouds race across the shapely peak of Cnicht whose western ridge sweeps down to Croesor, a village forever associated with the slate industry, which has formed such an integral part of the history and heritage of this region.

Moorland wilderness
Arenig Fawr and Moel Llyfnant
stretch across the skyline
beyond the Migneint, a vast
expanse of heather moorland
and blanket bog stretching
between Ffestiniog and Bala.

Autumn reflections
A patchwork of autumn colours reflected in the calm waters of Llyn Tegid near Bala.

Dark skies
Storm clouds sweep across
the sand dunes at Harlech. The
curve of the sandy beach leads
the eye towards Porthmadog.

Dune
Sand dunes form an important part of the Snowdonia coastal landscape near Llanbedr.

Menacing storm
Menacing storm clouds
sweep across Cardigan Bay
as the sun sets beyond the
Lleyn Peninsula in this view
from near Llanfair.

The Rhinog hills
The imposing Rhinog Fawr and Rhinog Fach on the skyline dominate the scene from the road to Maes-y-garnedd at the head of Cwm Nantcol. The deep cleft between the hills is Bwlch Drws Ardudwy, through which an old drover's road passed.

Craggy slopes
Boulders act as a pleasing foreground in this view of the dramatic buttresses of Penygadair soaring up above Llyn Cau.

Cwm Cau
A snow dusted Pen y Gadair, the high point of the Cader Idris massif, overlooks Cwm Cau, situated above Minffordd on the southern flanks of Cader Idris. The cwm is one of the finest in Wales.

Atmospheric dusk
An atmospheric winter shower, picked out by the setting sun, sweeps across the head of the Valley of the Afon Dysynni in this view from Craig yr Aderyn situated to the north-east of Towyn.

Bird Rock
The aptly named Craig yr Aderyn (Bird Rock) in the Dysynni Valley is the haunt of many species of birds including cormorants, which are normally coastal dwellers.

Gentle hills
The Tarren range of gentle hills seen here from the summit of Craig yr Aderyn (Bird Rock), bathe in the warmth of the setting sun.

A miniature gem
A beautiful winter morning with the small but shapely peak of Pared y Cefn-hir reflected in the mirror-like surface of Llynnau Cregennen near Arthog.

Snowy mantle
On a showery winter morning, the snow-capped Cader Idris range looks very beautiful in this view from the ridge of Pared y Cefn-hir overlooking Llynnau Cregennen.

Standing stone
An ancient standing stone backed by Tyrrau Mawr, one of the peaks on the western flanks of the Cader Idris range.

Tyrrau Mawr at dusk
A summer sunset warms the western slopes of Tyrrau Mawr seen here reflected in the calm surface of Llynnau Cregennen.

131

Mawddach Estuary
In this evening view west across Mawddach Estuary from the rugged hillside of Dinas Oleu, above Barmouth, the evening sunshine picks out the Cader Idris range.

Red sky at night
The setting sun creates a
dramatic view over the
Mawddach Estuary.

A Torrent Walk

The Afon Clywedog, which is overlooked from the footpath on the popular Torrent Walk near Dolgellau, rushes between glistening rocks. A long exposure emphasises the movement of the water creating a silky veil.

Across the bay
Yr Eifl (The Rivals) seen from
the west across the beach
at Porth Dinllaen.

Sea and hills
The ruins of the hillfort of
Tre'r Ceiri provide a fine view
over the northern Lleyn towards
Caernarfon. The gentle hills
of Moel Pen-Llechog and Gyrn
Ddu overlook the coastline.

Golden beach
A beautiful spring morning as the sea rolls into Porth Dinllaen, a stunning bay on the north side of the Lleyn Peninsula.

End of the day
The afterglow of the setting sun creates a peaceful scene in this view of sea
and boulders near Llanbedr, with the Snowdonia hills on the distant horizon.